JOAN AND FEYNE WEAVER

EVERYMAN'S GUIDE TO...
DOWN UNDER

ILLUSTRATED BY JEFF HOOK

RIGBY

WELDON·HARDIE
GROUP OF COMPANIES

Published by Rigby Publishers,
a division of RPLA Pty Limited
176 South Creek Road, Dee Why West, NSW 2099

First published 1984
Reprinted 1985, 1986
Copyright © Joan Weaver, Feyne Weaver, and Jeff Hook
Wholly designed and typeset in Australia
Printed in Hong Kong by Everbest Printing Co. Ltd

National Library of Australia
Cataloguing-in-Publication entry

Weaver, Joan, 1946–
  Everyman's guide to down under.
  ISBN 0 7270 1914 7.
  1. Australia – Description and travel – 1976 –
  – Guide-books. I. Weaver, Feyne, 1943– . II. Hook,
  Jeff, 1928– . III. Title.
919.4'0463

INTRODUCTION

G'day. So you're thinking of visiting Down Under (or you're already here)? Welcome. This book will be an invaluable guide to the customs, language and expressions, habits, and foibles of Australians. It will explain our currency, our accents . . . in fact, everything you need to know—and a lot you probably don't want to know.

Mind you, we've included only the most common bits of information—to include them all would mean fifteen volumes weighing three tonnes, and three very tired authors.

It may even help with getting to know our wildlife, which can easily be seen in our pubs near closing time, and not so easily in bushland. And this book will also be handy in carrying out the Great Australian Salute (see under 'G').

Whatever you want to know for your visit Down Under, may we (with a flourish and a fanfare) say humbly—look no further! All the answers are here, so please pay the cashier.

AUSTRALIA

What is Australia like, you ask. Well, in a lot of ways it is like the 51st state of the U.S. Everywhere you look there is Kentucky Fried, Coca Cola, Pepsi, Safeway, K Mart, 7-Eleven, McDonalds, Wendys, Dennys, Hertz, Holiday Inn, blue jeans, and cowboy boots.

But there are two big differences—we drive on the wrong side of the road, and, according to your countrymen, we talk funny.

Australia is multi-cultural, with many religions. In Melbourne during winter, football is probably the biggest religion (see 'Foody'). And there's another thing. We have summer at Christmas time (or Christmas in the summer . . . depending on which way you look at it).

And we flick our light switches down to turn them on, and up to turn them off. Our power points have an on-off switch, and our electricity is 240 volts. Our entrance and exit doors in stores are reversed to those in America; and no, the plumbing hasn't gone haywire—the toilet bowl never gets more water in it than that.

Many of the words and expressions used by Australians mean just the opposite, and . . . if you're beginning to think that everything here is upside down, remember . . . you *are* Down Under.

By the way—it's going to cost you $20 departure tax to get out of our country. But, there are those who would gladly pay $200 for the chance.

AUSTRALIANS

Generally, Australians are a friendly lot, but they do not suffer fools gladly.

And they are not a demonstratively patriotic race. Heavens no! In fact, most Aussies are the first to 'knock' their country. But may we suggest that you don't agree with them. Because that is when they *do* become patriotic. And occasionally they emphasise each point—violently.

Most Australians are also a hard-drinking lot. If you drink with them, you're a 'good bloke' (you're holding a 'dictionary'—use it). And if you buy the beer, you are a 'bonzer bloke'. On the other hand, if you don't buy a beer, you are a 'bludger'.

We'd like to be able to say *all* Australians are hard workers, but so many bludgers makes it difficult to say that with a straight face. Now, while we are just slightly ahead of the lynch mob, we would hasten to add that your 'fair dinkum' Aussie *is* indeed, a hard-working person. If the Aussie is a man, he's also a hard-playing, hard-drinking person, with a sense of fair play and a tendency to support the underdog.

Most Australians are also sports-minded and if they can't play a sport, they at least follow it.

A true Australian has four pet hates—bludgers, whingers, interstate beer, and bureaucracy. And, more often than not, a fifth pet hate is 'bloody Poms'.

ACCENT

A

ACCENT Now you know, and we know, that *you* are the ones with the accent. However, there are a couple of things . . . for example, you will find that Australians don't sound the 'r' in words: beer is 'beea'; weather is 'weatha'. Also the 'ay' sound usually comes out (to your ear) as 'eye'. So 'mate' sounds like 'mite'; play sounds like 'ply'. Then there is the 'eye' sound—it becomes 'oy'. Crikey becomes 'croikey'; light becomes 'loit'. And let's not forget words like 'new' and 'nuclear'—our pronunciation is 'nyew' and 'nyewclear', as opposed to your 'noo' and 'nooclear'.

Now you are getting it roit . . . and keep at it mite. Nevva sye doy.

AIRLINES Australia is serviced by all major world airlines (when we're not having an oil-tanker drivers' strike, air traffic controllers' strike, ground crew strike, or a flight crew strike).

Our two main domestic airlines are TAA and Ansett, serving all capital cities and some provincial cities (when there are not oil-tanker drivers' strikes, air traffic controllers' strikes, ground crew strikes, or flight crew strikes). Most country (or bush) runs are left to smaller commuter air services.

All airports are serviced by buses (coaches) to and from the city. They are cheaper, but cabs are quicker . . . sometimes. It all depends on the traffic, you see, and whether the trams and trains are on strike.

ALICE; THE ALICE This is the affectionate name for the town of Alice Springs in central Australia, and not the name of a local girl that you should get to know. The Alice is very hot and dry—in fact it is so dry that the annual Henley-on-Todd boat regatta is held in the dry bed of the Todd River. The boats have 'legs', you see.

ALUMINIUM   We pronounce it 'al-yew-mini-um'. You pronounce it . . . well, *you* know how you pronounce it, and you know how to spell it too!

'ANGON   Wait.

APPLES   Okay; all right. 'Ah, she'll be apples'—'she' being the situation in question. Everything in Australia is a 'she'—except women.

ARISTOTLE   Rhyming slang for bottle (see under 'R').

ARSE   This is our equivalent of your 'ass'. It also means luck. If someone wins some money they will be referred to as an 'arsy barst'd' or 'talk about arse'. However, to 'get the arse' means to 'get the sack'.

ARSE-END   This has two meanings: the pits, or the rear.

ARVO   Afternoon.

AVAGO   A general exhortation, but often associated with sport where a supporter will shout (scream might be a better word) 'Avago ya bluddy mug'—meaning the player should 'have a go'. But, believe it or not, that spectator is supporting that player. Really!

AXED   Fired, sacked, dropped (from a sports team).

AY   This can mean three things, depending on the tone of voice used. It can mean 'Hey, you'; 'Pardon?'; or 'Watch it!'. Try not to confuse the last two and you should have a healthy stay.

AYERS ROCK   The world's largest monolith, it is near Alice Springs. You can't miss it.

B

BANG-ON   Correct.

BARBIE   Barbecue. This summertime ritual is staged in much the same way as you have a barbecue, except we usually share ours with millions of flies.

BARNEY   Fight. As you progress through these pages you will see there are a lot of words for 'fight'. In fact, there are more words than there are fights.

A BARBIE

TRUMPET FOR SOUNDING DURING MOMENTS OF TRIUMPH

BEANIE IN CLUB COLORS

NAME and NUMBER ⊂ FAVORITE PLAYER

ESKY (CAR FRIDG⸮ CONTAINING SURVIVAL KIT (COLD BEER)

SCARF IN CLUB COLORS

LEG WARMERS IN CLUB COLORS

BARRACKER (FOOTBALLUS FANATICUS)

BARRACK This has absolutely nothing to do with accommodation for soldiers. It means to support, cheer, root for, as in sport.

BARST'D (Bastard) Might we suggest this be approached with a certain amount of caution? You see, this word can be both a term of endearment and an insult. If you are called 'a stupid barst'd' with a chuckle, the speaker is being nice. If he says the same thing minus the chuckle, he's not being nice. If he says 'you rotten

10

barst'd' with something of a surprised tone, he is joking with you. If he says it in a level tone, he isn't—joking, that is.

BATHERS People who go to the beach or swimming pools, obviously. But it is also the name given to swimming costumes.

BATHS You will hear this a lot in the summer. Everybody is 'going to the baths'. We're not all washing together, nor is it that we're madly keen on scrubbing ourselves. (Mind you, everyone will tell you we bathe more than the Poms.) Bath refers to public swimming pools.

BEEA (Beer) Never order a glass of beer like you do back home. No, no. Here you must ask for a 'glarse of beea'. And the same with light beer. If you ask for a 'lart beer' all you will get is a funny look. You must pronounce it 'loit beea'. A can or bottle is referred to as 'a coldie'. A can is also often referred to as 'a tinny'.

BELT-UP Shut up (also see 'Taxis').

BEWDY (Beauty) Good.

BEWDY-BOTTLER Very good. If it is, in fact, excellent, the expression is usually 'rip-snorter'. You are starting to get the hang of this strange language, aren't you?

BIG SMOKE Refers to a big city. Very appropriate when you consider air pollution these days.

BIKE Bicycle, pushbike. It can also mean a local girl you shouldn't get to know.

BIKIE You call them bikers. Generally it's a good idea to call them 'Sir'.

BIKKIES Short for biscuits. Also means money, hence 'big bikkies', a lot of money.

BILLY Usually a large tin can fitted out with a wire handle, and used for brewing tea over a campfire (see 'Tea'). Swaggies (see under 'S') use these mostly because they can't afford anything else.

BINGLE A crash.

BIRD A girl, or an attractive woman.

BIRDWATCHING Certainly a favourite past-time this, watching all the birds walk by. There are, of course, some strange people who actually like watching real birds of the feathered variety.

BISCUITS Concentrate now—this is not going to be easy for either of us. A biscuit here, is what you call a cookie. What you call a biscuit, we call a scone. What you call a scone, we call a bun. What we call . . . don't call us, we'll call you!

BLINDER A great effort.

11

BIRDS!

BLOCK   For the doing of. 'He did his block'—he lost his temper.

BLOKE   A guy, a man. It rhymes with 'poke'.

BLOODHOUSE   See 'Hotels'.

BLOWER   A telephone. And they are called public phones, not pay phones. But believe us—you pay. It is 20 cents for local calls and we shudder at the cost of trunk (long distance) calls.

BLUDDY   (Bloody) This, friends, is the great Australian adjective. It is used everywhere, including to punctuate normal speech. For example: 'There I bluddy was, mindin' me own bluddy business, drivin' along the bluddy highway, when this bluddy great kanga-bluddy-roo hopped across the bluddy road straight in bluddy front o' me. Well, kiddin' I didn't hit the bluddy skids [brakes]. No bluddy risk, sport.'

BLUDDY HELL   Gosh; damn it. There's more, but you get the i-bluddy-dea now, doncha cobber.

(Like) BLUDDY HELL   No.

BLUDDY OATH   Yes.

BLUDGE   A job with practically no work; to do nothing. To borrow without intending to repay.

BLUDGER   One who does the above; such a one is not greatly admired. Also used as an insult.

BLUE   A fight. Also a nickname for a redhead.

BLUEY   A parking ticket or a summons. Also the name given to a hobo's pack (see 'Swaggie').

BOMB   An old car.

BOMBED   Fell flat; 'The show bombed'. Now, bearing in mind that Australians are a great beer-drinking race, 'bombed' also means 'drunk'.

BONKERS   Crazy.

BONZER   Good. 'He's a bonzer bloke' means 'he's a good guy' or 'a good ol' boy'.

BOWLS   Ah yes, well, this is nothing like ten-pin bowls (which we do have here). This is played on a lawn which is called 'a rink'. There is a little white ball called the kitty (would we lie to you?) and the idea is for the bowler to get his big black bowl, which is biased (well, who isn't these days?) closest to the kitty. His opponent has the same idea, and can try to knock his bowls out of the way. The game is not over until all the ends are over, sorry, ended . . . er . . . played. Then . . . you don't really want to know about all this, do you?

13

BOX BROWNIE   Used in reference to a lower and delicate portion of a woman's anatomy. Also used as a general term for camera.

BRASS RAZOO   As in 'I haven't got a brass razoo'—'I haven't got a cent'.

BREWER'S DROOP   How can we put this delicately? Um . . . we all know that beer affects a man's . . . shall we say . . . sexual prowess. And when a man has had too much to drink, he can't . . . ah . . . rise to the occasion, so to speak. Really, the term is quite self-explanatory when you think about it.

BRUMBIE   Wild horse (you call them mustangs).

BRUMMY   Faulty item.

BUGGER   Another term of endearment—that is, if they say 'ya silly bugger'. But if they say 'bugger you', don't smile. And if they tell you to 'bugger off' . . . well, if we were you, we'd bugger off.

BUGGER ALL   Nothing; 'I've got bugger all' (money).

BUGGER ME   Well, I'll be blowed.

BUGGER OFF   Leave . . . as in immediately.

BULLEMAKANKA   This is the legendary town where everyone who has 'gone walkabout' (see under 'W') ends up—'He's gone to Bullemakanka'. It also refers to anywhere that is a long distance from the city, usually in the outback (see under 'O'), the name of which the speaker is unsure.

BUM   The behind or bottom. It has nothing to do with tramps or vagrants.

BUSH   Country. If someone says 'he's gone bush', they mean the person in question has gone to the country. Country towns are referred to as 'bush towns'. If someone says he is bushed, have a good look at him—because it can mean he is exhausted, or he is lost.

BUT   Used mainly at the end of a sentence by people from New South Wales, Queensland, and Western Australia. 'It's a nice day, but' . . . they are not going to continue with 'I don't like it' or some such thing. They actually have finished their statement, but.

C

CAFE Pronounced 'kaffay'. These are a bit like American coffee shops, except they don't serve alcohol.

CAKE HOLE Mouth.

CARDIGAN Also called a cardie—that's a jacket to you. And jumpers here are sweaters, or pullovers, to you.

CARNA Come on, but usually associated with barracking for your sporting team, as in 'Carna Magpies'.

CARN Come on.

CHAR Tea.

CHEMIST Druggist, pharmacist.

CHEWY Chewing gum.

CHEQUE You spell it check, but it still means money.

CHINA Part of the rhyming slang 'china plate'—mate.

CHLOE Ah, beautiful Chloe! No visit to Melbourne is complete without seeing Chloe. Beautiful, naked Chloe. Calm down—it's just a famous painting in Young and Jackson's Hotel. A cabbie can take you to it.

CHOOK Hen, as in chicken or even as in old lady.

CHOP 'Give it the chop'—get rid of it. Or 'get in for your chop'—get your share.

CHUNDER This is actually the act of vomiting after a night on the slops (see 'Drinking')—sometimes a part of the 10 o'clock swill (see 'Hotel'). It is also known by many other names hence, any respectable Australian dictionary would carry the entry: 'Vomit—to spew, chunder, perk, growl at the grass, a technicolour yawn, heave one's guts up, chuck, lay a pizza, liquid yodel.'

CITIES Obviously each Australian state has a capital city. In each case, it is the biggest city in each state. Melbourne is the capital of Victoria; Sydney—New South Wales; Adelaide—South Australia; Perth—Western Australia; Brisbane—Queensland; Hobart—Tasmania; Darwin—Northern Territory; and Canberra—Australian Capital Territory. Each state has provincial cities, and despite the fact that some of them are quite large, they're still referred to by people living 'in the big smoke' as being 'in the bush'.

The cities, like towns, are a mixture of office buildings,

department stores, small stores, cafes, restaurants, newsagents, and so on. Therefore, while large shopping centres are scattered around the suburbs, you can do the same type of shopping in the 'downtown' area . . . if you can find a parking spot (see 'Grey ghosts').

Now, if you are in Melbourne, don't praise Sydney, and vice versa. Indeed no. There is a terrible amount of rivalry between Australia's two biggest cities, and some violent scenes have been witnessed over the years when antagonists from the two places have got together. Horrible! Why this should be is anybody's guess, when you consider that Sydney isn't a patch on Melbourne . . . (or is that, Melbourne isn't a patch on Sydney?).

Sydney generally has a nice climate, although it can get very humid. Brisbane is humid for much of the time, but not uncomfortably so. Adelaide has a good climate and is rarely humid. Darwin is *hot* and often humid. Perth has beautiful weather. Melbourne has weather—all kinds and just about every day. There is a saying that if you don't like the weather in Melbourne—wait five minutes. Hobart, way down there, can be very cold.

But who cares about the weather when there are many magnificent sights like . . . well there is . . . and . . . then there's . . . um, well, the beer is good.

CLAPPED OUT Ruined, or useless. Usually used in reference to an old car.

CLOBBER Clothing. It can, however, mean to hit. As in: 'Do that again ya bluddy mug, and I'll clobber ya.'

CLOT An idiot.

COAT-HANGER This is Melbourne's affectionate nickname for the Sydney Harbour Bridge. Sydney responds by calling Australian Rules Football 'aerial pingpong'.

COBBER A friend; mate.

COCK-UP Something's gone wrong again.

COCKY A farmer. It can also mean a person is over-confident. And believe it or not, it is also used as a shortened version of 'cockatoo', a parrot.

COLDIE A cold can or bottle of beer.

COME OFF IT This is not to suggest that anyone is on it. The term means 'don't lie' or 'don't exaggerate' or 'I don't believe you'.

CONSTABLE This is a policeman of the bottom rank. You call them officers. It is pronounced (correctly) as it is spelt, but

17

Australians have a tendency to pronounce it 'cunstible', which may very well reflect what they think of them. Other ranks are senior constables, sergeant, senior sergeant, superintendent, and inspector.

COP SHOP   A police station, or precinct.

CORKER   Good. 'It was a corker movie'—it was a good movie.

COW COCKY   A dairy farmer.

CRACK-A-COLDIE   To open a can or bottle of beer.

CRANK   An idiot.

CRICKET   Strange sport, this. There are eleven players in each side, and the team on the oval (arena) is out, while the team that is in, is in the dressing room except for the two batsmen who are out on the field.

The team that is out tries to get the team that is in, out, so they can go in. To do this they must bowl the batsmen out, run them out, catch them out, or get them out lbw (leg before wicket).

The batsman stands at the end of the pitch which is twenty metres long, and tries to hit the ball which the bowler sends down. The bowler must use an over-arm, straight-arm action. He is not allowed to throw the ball. And the ball should bounce on the pitch before it gets to the batsman. If the batsman misses the ball and it hits his stumps (three sticks stuck in the ground), he is out. If he hits the ball in the air and a fieldsman catches it before it hits the ground, the batsman is out.

To score runs, the batsmen (there are two in together) must run from end to end of the pitch before the fielding side can get the ball and hit the stumps. If a batsman is out of his crease (a line on the ground in front of the stumps) and the fieldsman hits the stumps with the ball, the batsman is run out.

If the ball hits the batsman on the pads (which protect his legs) and the umpire reckons that the ball would have hit the stumps if the batsman hadn't been there (where else would he be?), then he's given out as lbw 'leg before wicket'. If a batsman fails to score a run, he is said to have 'made a duck'. If he 'makes a duck' in both innings, he is said to have 'made a pair'.

When ten batsmen are out, and back in the pavilion, the whole side is out and the other team goes in—and the whole complicated mess starts again.

The winner is decided by who makes the most runs. If the ball reaches the boundary it is four runs. If it is hit in the air over the

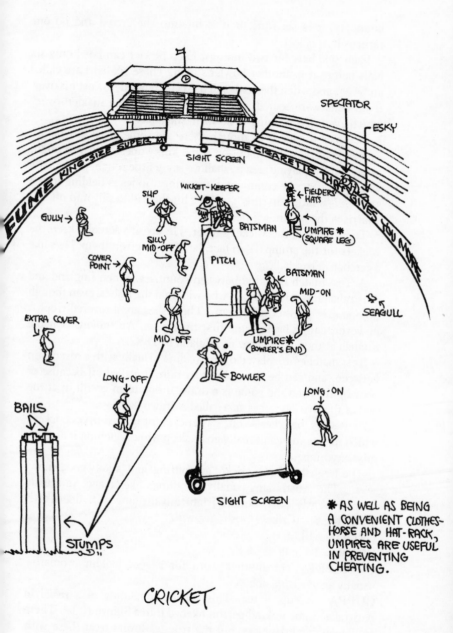

CRICKET

boundary, it is six runs. If it is hit into the crowd and no one returns it, it is lost.

Each side bats for two innings. Each bowler can bowl only six balls before it is another bowler's turn. These six balls are called an 'over', and when the sixth ball has been bowled, the over is over. If no runs were scored, the bowler has 'bowled a maiden over', which event has nothing to do with 'sheilahs'.

At times it sounds as though there are some physically handicapped players, not to mention some kinky ones. And you might think that the playing area is, shall we say, a little rough, particularly when you hear the commentators saying: 'Jones is fielding in the gully' . . . 'Smith is in slips' . . . 'He's hit the ball to silly mid-off' . . . 'Harris is the square-leg fieldsman'.

Then there is the wicket keeper. He doesn't actually keep the wickets (or the stumps)—in fact, he is never given them. He's like a catcher in baseball.

A Test match is played between countries. When England and Australia play, it is to decide who will hold the Ashes, even though no one ever gets to hold them. (The Ashes are a revered trophy, however, dating back to the first time when Australians beat the English at their own game in England in 1882.)

Test matches are played over five days, usually with a rest day in between, and can be washed out by rain, or called off because of poor light. Then the game is a draw. If one team is still in at the end of the five days, it is also called a drawn game.

Nowadays there is also one-day cricket (or limited-overs cricket), which means you can't really go to sleep while watching it and not miss anything.

The English refer to cricket as 'spiffing' and 'a jolly good show, what'. The Australians usually say things like 'avago, ya bluddy mug' or 'bewdy sport'. Sounds frightfully thrilling stuff, doesn't it?

CROIKEY   (Crikey) Gosh; gee whiz.

CROOK   Ill.

CROW   To brag.

CRUMPET   Yet another word for a good-looking woman— usually an available one.

CUPPA   A cup of tea. This can be something of a ritual in Australia. Some unkind person likened it to a Shintu ritual. There are jigglers and danglers, but the true tea-lovers treat these with disdain.

CROOK

Uttering strange incantations like 'one for each person, and one for the pot', they spoon loose tea-leaves into The Tea Pot. Then comes 'take the pot to the kettle' as they carry The Tea Pot to the kettle and pour in boiling water.

The tea must, of course, be left standing 'to brew'. Finally, a Tea Strainer is placed over each cup as the holy nectar is poured from the Tea Pot, which must be covered by a Tea Cosy to keep the tea 'just right'.

And with the first sip, they utter: 'Ah, that's better.' Better than what, we wonder.

CURLY Nickname for someone with straight hair, or a bald person. It can also mean tricky. 'That's a curly one'—that's a tricky question.

CURRENCY You will be pleased to know that Australia's currency is the same as America's—dollars and cents. But the money is vastly different in appearance, and what it is called.

Certainly dollars are called bucks, and *some* of the slang names may be the same. But generally, money is called moolah, dough, bread, ready (as in ready cash), spondooli, loot, bread-and-honey, bikkies, lolly. It can also be called: dollar—half a quid; two dollars—a quid; 5¢ piece—zack; 10¢ piece—deena; 20¢ piece— two bob. These date back to pre-1966 when Australia's currency was in pounds, shillings, and pence, and relate to that currency's modern equivalent. For example, a sixpenny piece (now 5¢) was the zack; one pound (a quid) is now $2.

Our notes, also known as funny money or Monopoly money, are: $1 (brown), about the same size as the U.S. note; $2 (green), slightly bigger than the $1 note—in fact, the bigger the denomination, the bigger the note (no wonder we stopped at the $50 note); $5 (purple); $10 (blue); $20 (red); $50 (yellow-green).

And they are called notes, not bills. A bill here is a demand for payment.

Our coins, too, start with the smallest, the 1¢ piece, and increase in size according to value. The copper coins are 1¢ and 2¢. Silver coins are 5¢, 10¢, 20¢ (no quarters asked or given here, sport), and 50¢ which also happens to have twelve sides, although you may get an old round one sometimes.

And, if you are wondering what the designs are—so did we for a while. Actually, they are part of Australia's fauna . . . lizards, platypuses, and so on (see 'Wildlife').

D

DACKS Trousers.

DAFT Stupid.

DAG A humourist.

DAMPER A loaf of bread made by bushmen from flour, water, and salt. They swear by it. We swear about it—it tastes awful!

DANDY In South Australia, that's what they call a small icecream in a cardboard 'bucket'.

DEENA See 'Currency'.

DELI Short for delicatessen.

DICK-HEAD A fool.

DIDDEE Did he? As in: 'Wha' diddee say?'.

DIGGER An Australian soldier. Also used as a friendly greeting instead of mate: 'G'day Digger'.

DILL Someone who is stupid.

DIN Noise.

DINK To take a 'passenger' on a bicycle.

DINKUM, DINKY-DI True, real.

DINNEE Didn't he. As in: 'He said yer a mug, dinnee'.

DINNER Many people still refer to lunch as dinner. And to dinner as tea. Ah yes, breakfast is still breakfast.

DIXIE This is what the small icecream in a cardboard 'bucket' is called in Victoria.

DOAN Don't.

DOANCHA Don't you.

DOB To dob in, to inform on.

DOLLY-DANGLERS Used more often than not in reference to Italians or Greeks, since they insist on hanging dolls of various types in every conceivable place in their cars.

DONK A car engine.

DOON Doing. As in: 'Watcha doon?'.

DOPE A drip. Yes, it is also used in connection with drugs.

DRESS Australians generally try to keep up with world fashions, whether they're good or bad. But the traditional image of an Australian man's casual summer garb is indeed a sight to behold. More so if he is off to the cricket for the day, because that's when

24

he can be seen in *all* his refinery—baggy shorts, singlet or T-shirt, floppy hat, zinc cream on his nose, rubber thongs on his feet, and an Esky in his hand (see 'Esky').

DRIVING   One of the first things you will notice if you intend driving in Australia is that the steering wheel is on the right (wrong)-hand side of the car. You certainly would have noticed this first had you got in the left-hand side of the car and prepared to take-off.

The reason the steering wheel is where it is, is because you are supposed to drive on the left-hand side of the road. This could explain some of the yells, and waving of fists, you have had from other motorists—they were not just being friendly.

Here, left is right, and right is wrong, as opposed to America where right is right and left is wrong. We also give way to traffic on our right, although the way some Australians drive, it might be wise to give way to everyone.

Your pedals are in the same order, but the steering column controls are reversed—but you probably noticed this when you went to indicate you were turning and the windscreen wipers came on.

Your speedometer is in kilometres per hour and the road speed-limit signs are in kilometres, and you are supposed to obey them—even if most Australian drivers don't. Road distances are, naturally enough, also in kilometres—except the ones that still haven't been changed.

When you want to refuel your car, you go to a service station not a gas station—although they do now sell gas . . . as in gas, not gasoline. Here you ask for petrol, not gas, and 'oyle' (oil) for the motor. You also ask to have the 'toyers' (tires) pumped up—if they're flat, that is.

Other things you need to know about your vehicle: fenders are called mudguards; trunks are called boots (don't ask why); hoods are called bonnets; and glove compartments are called glove boxes.

The driving age varies from state to state—for example, in South Australia it is sixteen; in Victoria, eighteen. If you are in doubt, ask a cabbie.

Happy motoring, and remember—keep left and you'll be right.

DRONGO   A dill.

DUFFER   Pay attention, you little duffers, you. This word has a couple of meanings. 'Duffer' is our word for rustler—so a cattle

A DRONGO.

duffer is what you call a cattle rustler. But it can also mean someone is silly, usually used affectionately in much the same way as we say 'you silly little sausage'.

DUMMY Apart from the obvious meaning of this word, it is also the name of that thing that parents shove into the mouths of howling babes to shut 'em up. You call it a pacifier.

DUNCE-OUT To miss out.

DUST-UP A fight.

DYE Day, as in 'Todye is Mundye, not Chewsdye' (Tuesday). So remember, if someone wants to know 'where are you going todye?', he's not morbidly asking after your place of future death.

E

EATING OUT This can be a frightfully tricky business. Firstly, only licensed restaurants or hotel lounges can serve alcohol with your meals. Secondly, don't go looking for a glass of water to start the proceedings, because that doesn't happen here. Thirdly, ordering your meal can leave you starving or overfed. Why? You might well ask. It's because our main course is your entrée; our entrée is your appetiser, although we too, have appetisers, but they're different to entrées—yours and ours. If you get that lot sorted out, you'll be pleased to know that desserts are called desserts, or sweets.

Now coffee—unless you are in a Dennys, or Wendys, you pay for every cup. And you have to ask for each cup. And white coffee means coffee with milk. You must specify if you want cream in the coffee instead of milk. But don't ask for creamer—we haven't got any (and see 'Tipping').

Oh, just in case you're an egg-eater, here an egg is an egg is an egg. If you want one sunnyside up, or over-easy, may we suggest a quick visit to the kitchen to cook it yourself? Otherwise, you get your eggs as they come—greasy, usually.

If you want a baked potato with sour cream, you must ask for an Idaho potato—please don't ask us why. And Dennys and Wendys are the only places that have heard of hash browns, even if they can't cook them properly.

EGG NISHNA   An air conditioner (see 'Strine').

EGG ON   To encourage.

EMMA CHIZZIT   How much is it?

ESKY   Friends, this is one of the most important things an Australian man can own. Also known as a car fridge, it goes everywhere with him—to the cricket or the football, or any outing for that matter. Why? Because it has got all his beer in it, with ice keeping it cold. And a man never goes anywhere without his 'coldies'.

EXPRESSIONS

He wouldn't work in an iron lung: This simply means that someone is lazy.

I'll have one for Ron: You have to be careful with this one, particularly if you are offering cigarettes. Someone might say 'I'll have one for Ron', and put the cigarette in his pocket. He is not taking it home to his mate named Ron. He is simply saving it for 'layda Ron' (later on). If he takes two—one to smoke now and one 'for Ron', tell Ron to go to blazes and grab one back.

Put it on the slate: Charge it. A request for credit.

Going to town: This is another of those clever little sayings that has more than one meaning. It can mean you are going into the city (nobody calls it a city when they can say they're going to town). It can also mean going the whole hog (going all-out).

Yeah, that'd be right: Meaning it isn't. Or you don't believe it.

Game as Ned Kelly: This is used to describe people who are not afraid of taking a few risks. Ned Kelly, of course was a famous (infamous) bushranger last century, who performed various daring deeds such as robbing people and shooting at Traps (police). Just how game he was is open to debate since he wore armour on his head and his body, and police bullets had a tendency to bounce off—until the law had the bright idea of shooting him in the legs ('well, cut me off at the knees and call me Shorty'), thus preventing him from making his usual escape.

Had the Richard: It is useless.

In ya boot: Go to hell.

Fair suck of the sauce bottle/sausage; fair crack of the whip; fair go: They all mean the same thing—give a man a break; give him a reasonable deal. For example, if your car was for sale and you

AN ESKY

thought it was worth $5000 and someone offered you $2000, your immediate reaction would be to say 'Fair suck of the sauce bottle'. Or it may be your second reaction, the first being to burst out laughing—or to hit him.

Sink the slipper: To kick someone, while wearing boots—never with slippers.

Put a sock in it: Be quiet; shut up.

Belt up: Shut up.

Don't come the raw prawn: Don't be an idiot; don't act dumb.

Rough end of the pineapple: Getting a bad deal.

Gone bush: Gone to the country.

Guest of the Government: A jail prisoner.

Tip the bucket: Insult someone, pointing out all his faults and then some. Also can mean to spill the beans (tell on someone).

Not worth two-bob: This originated in the days of the imperial currency of pounds, shillings, and pence. A two-shilling piece was known as two-bob (now 20 cents). Not worth two-bob meant it wasn't worth much. Also, *mad as a two-bob watch*: Erratic, unreliable, crazy.

Does that tickle your fancy?: And they never laid a hand on you. It means 'Do you like it?'

All over the road like a mad woman's breakfast: Usually used to describe erratic driving.

Mad as a meat-axe: How mad a meat-axe is has never been determined. Where this expression originated is anyone's guess, but it means that someone is indeed mad.

Like a bull at a gate: Rushing in headlong, not taking care. (Usually run together, 'bullattagate'). Similar to 'bull in a China shop'.

That's a monty: That's a certainty.

Ball and Chain: Usually a man's reference to his wife.

Like a rat up a drainpipe: Means that someone has gone somewhere in a great hurry.

In like Flynn: Means you are a certainty to achieve something. It refers to Errol Flynn (who was originally from Tasmania) and his chances with women, which apparently were always considered a certainty.

In the club: Pregnant.

You give me the pip: Nothing to do with lemons. It means you annoy me.

Off like a Bondi tram: Since Bondi doesn't have trams anymore, this is obviously an old saying referring to the speed with which they departed (the trams, that is). The expression means someone left in a great hurry.

Arf-a-mo: Wait a minute. It is not a reference to someone who shaved only half his face that morning.

Stone the crows: All that just to mean 'gosh'.

You've got Buckleys: This means you have no chance. The original expression was 'You've got two chances—Buckleys and none'. *Fat chance* means the same thing.

Like a house on fire: If a couple are getting on well together, they are 'getting on like a house on fire'. Dare we suggest this expression was prompted by the heat of passion?

Bob's your uncle: You probably don't even know anyone called Bob, let alone have an uncle by that name. So when someone tells you that Bob is, in fact, your uncle, please don't argue or whip out your family tree. They mean 'she's apples'—everything is okay.

Flat out like a lizard drinking: Simply, this means you are terribly busy.

Having a lend of you: Actually nobody has borrowed you. What they have done is pulled your leg—had a joke at your expense.

Dropped his bundle: To panic, to give up, to fall to pieces.

Got a wog: In this case, the wog does not refer to an Italian or Greek. No, it means a virus. So when someone is ill, he says he has 'got a wog'. Mind you, there has been a reported case of an Italian who, feeling ill, said he 'had an Australian'.

How-do-you-do: No one is being polite here. It is yet another expression for a fight. If two or more people are 'getting stuck into it' the commotion is referred to as 'a nice old how-do-you-do', but really there is nothing nice about it. It can also mean that someone has got themselves into a sticky situation; a problem that will be hard to solve.

Going like a stuck pig: Going very fast as, we imagine, a pig would if it had something stuck into it.

Going like the clappers: Also going very fast. This comes from how the 'clappers' in bells go when someone is swinging on the end of the bell ropes.

Crying poormouth: Now, this is sad. Someone who (sob) cries poormouth is saying how poor they are—and usually getting bugger-all sympathy.

31

STONE THE CROWS

Scream bluddy murder: Hang on, don't race ahead . . . this isn't what you think. It simply means yelling or screaming very loudly.
Up the creek: In trouble.
Up the proverbial (creek)*:* As in 'up the creek' (in trouble).
Up the creek without a paddle: Same as above, only worse.
Make book on it: To take bets on something. Can be used as a saying to emphasise that something is true.
Back-of-beyond: Now *that's* a long, long way.
Back o'Bourke: This is also a long, long way.
On the never-never: If someone obtains something 'on the never-never', they have bought something on hire purchase, or time payment. It is called the never-never because most people think that with the interest charged on hire purchase, you 'never-never' get it paid off. But we'd never, never suggest that companies charge too much interest . . .

F

FAGS   Cigarettes. Also known as cigs, OPs (other people's), cancer tubes or sticks, coffin nails, or smokes. Fags can also refer to homosexuals, so be careful who you ask for a fag. Come to think of it, better stick with any of the other choices.
FAIR DINKUM   True; really; honest; honestly; factual. Can be a query: 'Is that fair dinkum?'
FANNY   Please don't use this word in mixed company. It refers to the same area on a woman as you mean it—except it is *not* at the rear.
FIZZER   Something that fails to work; or succeed.
FLAG   Australia's national flag has the English Union Jack in the top left corner, with the Southern Cross star formation, plus the Star of the Commonwealth in white on a blue background.
FLAMIN'   This is sometimes substituted for the word 'bluddy'. But only sometimes, because to an Australian, there is nothing quite as satisfying as having a good swear.

FLAT   Apart from the obvious, it also means an apartment.

FLICKS   The movies.

FLOOZY   A woman of loose morals.

FOODY   Footy; short for football. This is Australia's national game and is played between two sides of eighteen players each. Probably the easiest way to describe it is that it is a cross between rugby, soccer, and Gaelic football, played with an oval ball, on an oval ground.

Players are not allowed to run more than fifteen metres without bouncing the ball, kicking it, or hand-passing (no throwing—it must be punched from one hand to the other). The general idea is that once a team is in possession of the ball, that team tries to keep things that way until they have scored a goal—by kicking the ball between the two tallest flagpoles at the end of the oval.

Players must not trip each other, push each other in the back, grab each other around the neck, grab another player when he hasn't got the ball, or fight. But they always do all of these things, which is why there are two umpires on the ground. The umpires are generally called 'yer bluddy mug' by the spectators.

When men in white coats and wearing white hats, and standing between the flagpoles start waving white flags, that does not mean they surrender. It means one of the teams has scored a goal or a behind. A goal is worth six points. A behind is worth one point—which is why a behind is often called a point; the crowd will often suggest a player should be kicked in the behind for kicking a behind.

Field positions: There are forwards and backs. Actually there are pockets and wings, too . . . may we suggest that, if you are really interested, you buy a proper rule book.

That's the game of foody. But the spectators are harder to work out. Everybody barracks (supports, roots for) a team, although it is often hard to figure which team they are supporting. If one of their own players doesn't seem to be pulling his weight, they will yell 'avago, ya bluddy mug'. Members of the opposing team are usually referred to as mongrels, morons, cheats, show ponies, and girls.

Other spectators are also referred to as mongrels, bluddy mugs, one-eyed, blind, of dubious parentage, and totally ignorant—as in: 'What would you know, yer bluddy no-hoper mug. Yer wouldn't know one end of a footy from the other'.

FOOTPATH   You call them sidewalks.

FOSTERS Probably Australia's best-known beer. But, every state has its own beers. In New South Wales there's Toohey's, Tooth's, or Resch's. In Western Australia the favourite seems to be Swan Lager; in South Australia it's West End, Southwark, or Coopers; Tasmania has Cascade; the Northern Territory has NT Draught in their idea of 'stubbies'—bottles that hold 2·25 litres. In Queensland, the best-known beer is XXXX, usually called 4 Ex; because the beer was called XXXX is not to suggest that, when it was first brewed and needed a name, no one could read or write!

F'REAL As in: 'Is that f'real?—Is that for real?

FREEBY Anything that is free.

FREEWAYS Bit of a joke, really. They're actually bottle-necks when it comes to peak-hour traffic. Perhaps they'll finish them one day . . .

FRENCH DRESSING Here it is usually a vinegar and oil-based dressing.

FREVVA Forever.

FRIGATE And there's not a ship in sight. Simply it means 'the hell with it'.

G

GACK A mess. And 'Gacky'—messy.

GALAH A fool, a gink; also a type of cockatoo (see 'Wildlife').

GAMBLING Australians love to gamble. Next to drinking, they probably love gambling best. Most of all, they love drinking and gambling at the same time. They will bet on two flies crawling up a pub wall. When Princess Diana and Prince Charles had their first baby, offices throughout the country ran sweeps (gambling games) on what they would name the baby.

Sweeps are run in *every* office throughout Australia when it comes to that big horse race of the year—the Melbourne Cup.

Most gambling, such as small raffles, two-up, poker games, and so on, are illegal—which hasn't stopped anyone partaking yet.

GAMBLING

But there is plenty of legal gambling which keeps the Government's coffers full. There is the Totalizator Agency Board (TAB) which is similar to your betting shops. Through them you can bet on thoroughbred racing, harness racing (trotting), and greyhound racing, as well as football.

Then there's the Pools—where you bet on soccer. Lotteries are very popular, as is Lotto (Cross-Lotto or Tattslotto). This is a weekly game where you pick six numbers out of forty, then keep your fingers crossed. First prize, which is usually shared by two to twenty entries, is always more than $1 million.

Instant lotteries are popular, too, where one scratches away at a little card and stands to win between $2 and $10 000 on the spot. And we also have bingo.

For the habitual gambler, there are four casinos—one in Hobart (Tasmania), one in Alice Springs in central Australia, one in Darwin in the Northern Territory, and one in Launceston, also in Tasmania. And if things go as planned, we will soon see at least one more—in South Australia. New South Wales has 'em, but doesn't admit to it. They do, however, admit to poker machines (often called pokies).

Actually, wherever you go you can bet on being able to take a gamble on something.

GANDER   To look. 'Have a gander'—have a look.

GARN   Go on, as if in disbelief.

GASBAG   One who talks a lot—and we mean a lot.

GAWK   To stare.

GAY AND HEARTY   A party.

G'DAY   The usual greeting, 'Good-day'—even if it is a lousy day.

GINK   A fool, an idiot.

GIRL   A coward; weakness. Those that drink low-alcohol beer are often called 'girls' and the beer is called 'girls' beer'.

GOB   The mouth.

GOOD-OH   Right, okay.

GOON   A galah (as in gink).

GORN   Gone.

GOSH   Rarely used by Australians when an expletive deleted will suffice.

GREASY SPOON   This is an affectionate name for a not-so-clean cafe. They are also known as a 'Chew 'n' Spew'.

A GASBAG!

THE GREAT AUSTRALIAN SALUTE!

GREAT AUSTRALIAN SALUTE   There are flies in Australia — there are lots and lots of flies in Australia! And at times it seems that *all* are around *you*, particularly around your head.

And so there is a constant waving of the hand back and forth in front of the face — the Great Australian Salute. (Actually, a book in the hand covers a bigger area.)

GREETINGS   Australians will rarely say 'Hello' or 'How do you do'. No, their usual form of greeting is 'G'day' or 'Ow*ya*goin', orright?'. Which, when translated, simply means: 'How are you going, all right?' The common reply is: 'Orright, ow*you*goin'?' — All right. How are you going?

And they are not asking by which mode of transport you are travelling. They are referring to your general health. But don't ever tell them if you have an illness, because they couldn't care less. They just use the term as a greeting and expect you to tell them that you are fine.

Sometimes they will throw in the words 'sport' or 'cobber' or 'mate' — all three mean 'friend'.

When they are leaving, Australians never say 'Goodbye'. It is 'Seeya' or 'Seeya layda' (see you later) whether they intend to or not; or 'Ooroo'. Sometimes they will simply announce 'Well, I'm orf' and disappear. Don't think you have offended them.

Australians also say 'tata' a lot, pronounced 'tat-tah'. This is another form of goodbye. But if they say 'he's got the tatas' it means the poor soul to whom they are referring has gone around the bend, gone crazy.

Night is different again. Perhaps it has something to do with a full moon. But, particularly in the country, they say 'Goodnight' — when they first meet you. Don't think you have done something wrong and they are trying to get rid of you in a hurry. They say 'Goodnight' when they meet you and say it again when they really mean goodnight (goodbye). Sometimes they say 'Hooray' — although what they have to cheer about is anyone's guess.

GREY GHOSTS   Parking inspectors. Also — depending on which state you are in — known as Brown Bombers, Gestapo, Rogan's Heroes . . .

GRILL   You might broil steaks, we grill them. That is not to say we put them under a strong light, hit 'em with a rubber hose, and ask where they were on the night of the thirteenth. It is just that we use a different word, but the end result is the same.

41

GROG Booze, liquor.

GROTTY Dirty, awful.

GUNNA This has nothing whatsoever to do with weapons. It means 'going to', same as 'gonna'.

GUTSA Come a gutsa; to fall over, as in: 'He came a gutsa'.

GWANNA Goanna, a type of lizard. Also used to refer to a piano.

HEATER Nothing to do with guns. It is a gas or electric fire.

HOLIDAY Vacation. Also a recognised public holiday.

HOON Stupid; a trouble-maker.

HOOTER The nose. Also a car horn.

HOTELS Depending on the standard of these establishments, they are called hotels, pubs, or bloodhouses.

Generally speaking, it is the big posh places like the Hiltons and what-have-you for which we reserve the word 'hotel'. After all, we couldn't have the genteel and refeened ladeez and gennelmen visiting and/or staying in anything *but* hotels, now could we, what? (As the Poms would say—if they were asked, that is.)

The pubs—ah yes, the pubs. Now this is where you will see your fair dinkum Aussies, breasting the bar, getting into the slops, as beer is lovingly called, and generally having a great time—until they feel their heads the next morning.

Of these types of hostelries, there are drinking pubs and staying pubs. You can drink in a staying pub, but you can't stay in a drinking pub. Well, you can—but not to stay, if you get our meaning.

Pubs are divided into public bars, saloon bars, and lounges. They are all 'public' (open) bars, except you can't stand up to drink in the lounge. (You can't stand up anywhere if you've had too much to drink!) A point to remember—most 'public bars' are considered by Australian men to be for men only—this might save some embarrassment. Yes, Australia is one of the last bastions of chauvinism.

HOTELS — BLOODHOUSES

Bars are found only in hotels, unless it is a wine bar, in which case you can't buy beer. Some motels have bars, but usually for the use of guests only, or guests and their visitors . . . and at funny hours. But then, just about everything about Australia's liquor laws is funny—as in peculiar.

43

All pubs have bottle departments. Some have both walk-in and drive-in bottle departments, and while you can walk into a drive-in department, you can't drive into a walk-in department. Pubs and licensed grocers are the only places where you can buy packaged beer. But the licensed grocers close at 5.30 p.m. on weekdays and at noon on Saturdays. None are open Sundays. Pubs can open on Sundays for limited hours, and in some states packaged beer can't be sold on a Sunday. A cab driver can set you right regarding the laws of the state.

Now, when you are in a pub and drinking with a group of men friends, you're regarded as 'one of the boys'. If you are told 'It's your shout', don't stand on the bar and yell. What they mean is it's your turn to buy a round—a round being another drink for each member of the group you are with.

You could have some trouble ordering a beer. Remembering it is pronounced 'beea', you can order anything from a pot, a glarse (glass), a pint, ponies (and for Gawd's sake don't go around looking for a horse), middies, butchers and schooners, both of which have absolutely nothing to do with meat vendors or ships at sea. It all depends on which state you are in. (Ask a cabbie.)

Once upon a time, Australian hotels had what was known as 'the six o'clock swill'. It meant that, since pubs shut at 6 p.m., everyone ordered as much as they could afford five minutes before closing time, then scoffed the lot as quickly as they could before the publican announced 'time gentlemen, please', and proceeded to turf the lot out into the street. The people that is, not the beer.

Since then, of course, Australia has gained some semblance of civilisation and the pubs now don't close until 10 p.m. Unless they've got a special late license and/or they have entertainment. So now we have the 10 o'clock swill (also see 'Chunder').

In the big, modern staying pubs—sorry, hotels—and motels, most rooms have refrigerators (you have to make your own ice for mixed drinks), and tea and coffee-making facilities. Some have toasters, too. Very few hotels and motels have twenty-four hour coffee shops. Most don't have coffee shops. Some do have twenty-four hour room service.

And again, it is only the big, modern chain hotels that will have someone manning the reception desk all night, in case you want some general information; which you probably wouldn't get anyway.

We have saved the best for last—bloodhouses. Bloodhouses are so-named because one can usually set a clock by the regularity with which brawls break out. Bloodhouses are also places to avoid. (If you have any doubt about a pub, ask a cabbie.)

HYMIE   Reference to a Jewish person.

I

ICY POLES   We may have strange eating habits, but this does not refer to frozen sticks. They are what you call popsicles.

IFFY   Suspect; risky.

INNASTATE   Interstate.

INNATICK   In a tick, in a minute.

INNIT   Isn't it?

IOTA   Used to illustrate a lack of something; not knowing something; nothing. 'I don't give an iota'; 'I haven't got an iota'; 'I don't care one iota'.

IRISH   Called Micks, or Paddys, they come in for a terrible amount of ridicule in Australia. And *all* those Polack jokes you know, are told here as Irish jokes. (Did you hear about the Irish firing squad? . . . They formed a circle.)

IRON   Press; to iron a shirt.

IRON OUT   To flatten, as in one man knocking out another. Also to straighten out a problem.

IRRITS   Short for irritate or irritation, as in: 'You give me the irrits.'

J

JACK-UP   To refuse to co-operate; to stop being helpful.

JAFFA   A round candy. Their most popular use was to roll them down the aisles of the theatres during movies. But since most theatres have now carpeted their wooden floors, the use of the Jaffa in this way has died out. But they are still nice to eat—orange-flavoured candy filled with chocolate.

JAM   Jelly. Also a spot of bother, a sticky situation!

JELLY   Gello.

JEVVA   Did you ever? 'Jevva get in touch with Harry?'

JINKER   An old horse-drawn carriage.

JOHNS   Short for rhyming slang 'John hops'—cops; police.

JOKER   A guy; a man.

JUMBUCK   Sheep.

JUNKET   A free trip. Also a milk dessert.

K

KARK, KARK IT   Die, to die.

KERFUFFLE   A rumpus. And someone can be in a kerfuffle—totally disorganised, in a mess.

KICKED IT, KICK THE BUCKET   Died, to die.

KINDA   (Pronounced Ky-nda) Kind of.

KINDY   Kindergarten, play school.

KING DICK   Someone who thinks they're better than anyone else—and acts like it.

KNICKERS   Women's panties, actually. Strangely, it is also used as a term of derision.

KNOCKERS   Here's another one—two meanings that one really shouldn't get confused. A knocker is someone who continually finds fault with things—Australians are known as the world's best 'knockers'. And knockers are women's breasts—usually on the large side. And you can't knock that.

KNOW-ALL   Someone who claims to know everything (but more often than not, doesn't); a smart-alec.

KULCHA   (Culture) Australia may be a little behind in such matters as the arts of the cultural variety than longer-established countries, but we're getting there. Museums, art galleries, cultural centres—they're springing up everywhere. Every capital city has top-class establishments of that ilk.

As someone by the name of Sir Leslie Paterson once said: 'Culture? We've got culture up to our arses'. (Sorry about that, but he did say it.)

L

LAIR   A show-off; a would-be hood. Of course, it also means an animal's living place.

A LAIR!

LARK A prank; a practical joke; a bit of fun.

LARRIKIN A lair (as in show-off, etc.).

LAVATORY This is where one goes to relieve oneself. It is also known as the toilet, the loo, the dunny, the shouse, or where a man goes to 'point Percy at the porcelain'.

Ask where the John is, and you'll be introduced to a man called John. Ask for the can, and a cold tinny (see 'Beer') of Fosters will be stuck in your hand. The same applies if you say you want to visit the head — you'll be whisked off for a visit to Tweed Heads in New South Wales.

Social etiquette demands that you rarely say you are going to the loo, or dunny or whatever. Women go 'to powder their nose', while men usually wander off in search of 'the little boy's room'.

That, of course, is if you are at a mixed party of rather refined people. Anywhere else and the blokes are 'off for a leak' and the sheilas have 'gotta find the dunny'.

And the bathroom — that is where you take a bath, shower, or 'freshen up'.

LEAD BALLOON Usually a joke that falls flat; as in: 'It went over like a lead balloon'.

LEAGUE'S CLUBS Apart from the Sydney Harbour Bridge and the Opera House, Sydney, the capital of New South Wales also has something else that most other states would love — League's Clubs.

These clubs are something like large hotels, but without accommodation. There is beer, wines and liquor, and meals at lower than normal prices, plus top entertainment and, the cause of most of the envy from other states, poker machines. These are often referred to as 'pokies', 'one-armed bandits', or 'thievin' barst'd machines, but'.

Cities and towns throughout New South Wales have similar establishments, but the description of poker machines never changes.

LOAF The head; 'Use ya loaf'. Also mean to be lazy on the job (or off the job, for that matter). Take an unscheduled break — 'to have a loaf'.

LOAFER Obviously, one who loafs.

LOCK-UP Jail. (We prefer to spell it 'gaol'.)

LOLLY A slang word for money. 'Lolly' is also used for candy — 'I want a bag of lollies'.

LOOT Money—again (we are obsessed with the stuff).

LOTTERIES There are dozens of these. They vary from state to state. Ask a cabbie (also see 'Gambling').

LOUT A larrikin.

LUBRA An Aboriginal woman. It can be used as a derogatory statement to describe a woman with big lips, 'lubra lips'.

LUCKY COUNTRY A lot of people keep calling Australia the Lucky Country. They could be right—lucky if you can get a job; lucky if you can afford to buy a house; lucky if the trains run on time . . .

We think, however, they may be referring to the abundance of natural resources this country has—like good football players, tennis players, cricketers . . .

LUCKY LEGS This describes a girl with very thin legs—'Lucky they don't snap off at the knees and . . .'

MASSAGE PARLORS Some are, some aren't. The ones that aren't would be illegal if they were called what they really are.

And while we are on the subject (of places to stay away from, unless you're that way inclined) every city has 'em. In Melbourne, Fitzroy Street, St Kilda, and some surrounding areas would be a nice neighbourhood not to be in. Parts of Kings Cross, Sydney, are the same. Ask a cabbie.

MATE Buddy, pal, friend. It has nothing to do with boy–girl relationships. Every man's friend is his mate. 'Owya goin', mate?'

MATILDA A swag, bluey, pack. It's what a tramp carries—his few meagre belongings.

To 'waltz a Matilda' is to carry a swag. You may not believe it, but that's what our best-known song 'Waltzing Matilda' is all about.

MEAT PIE This is the great Australian dish. But it must have tomato sauce with it.

MIGRANTS These come in all shapes, sizes, and colours, and all claim to be Australian, even if they can't speak English, let alone Australian. They all have nicknames:

Italians: Eyeties, wogs, dagos or spags.

Greeks: Wogs or dagos.

Arabs (and other Middle East migrants): Wops.

Jews: Four-by-twos.

Blacks: Boongs, coons, niggers, Abos (if they are Australian Aborigines).

Americans: Yanks (wherever they come from), septic tanks (see 'Rhyming slang').

Chinese: Chinks.

Japanese: Nips.

Other orientals: Slants, slant heads.

French: Frogs.

English: Poms, whingin' Poms, or bluddy whingin' Poms. Sometimes also known as Pommie bastards.

Irish: Paddy or Mick.

New Zealanders: Kiwis.

Pakistanis: Pakis.

These are never used to one's face, unless one is trying to provoke a fight.

MILK BARS These are quaint little establishments, peculiar to Australia. We've known some peculiar Australians running these, too.

Milk bars are open long hours, seven days a week, and sell groceries, soft drinks, cigarettes, milk shakes, spiders (turn the page to 'S'—we're not going to explain that here), hosiery, pet food, bread, newspapers, take-away meals—'food to go'—(sandwiches, pies, etc.), and . . . oh, yes . . . milk. And this is where you can buy that bag of lollies.

MISSUS Mrs. Usually used by a man to refer to his wife—if he's being polite!

MONTY A certainty.

MOOLAH Money . . . (again!).

MUG A fool; also a metal cup.

MULGA Generally used to refer to the bush, the Outback—remote country areas. It is also a type of tree in the Outback.

MY OATH Yes; certainly . . . (sometimes shortened to 'bluddy oath').

N

NAMES We really are a dreadful race when it comes to names—we have absolutely no respect for them.

Firstly, we shorten them. If your name is Robert, you'll be called Bob, whether you like it or not. Or if it's Edward, you'll get Ed or Ted. And Anthony becomes Tony. Or they'll change them—totally—such as John to Jack. Get the idea?

But on top of that, Australians have a habit of sticking an 'ee' sound on the end of names of people and even objects. So you get Mickey, Bobby, Ricky, Jacky, Teddy, Scotty, Joanie, truckie (rather than trucker), and so on.

Bewdy, right?

NA-NAS Short for 'bananas', as in: 'He's gone nanas'.

NANNA This is derived from 'nanny', as in one who cares for children, rather than from the goat. Usually refers to a grandmother.

NAPPY A diaper.

NATTER To talk, chatter.

NEDDY A horse. 'Nag' is another word for the same poor unfortunate beast, as is 'gee-gee' (pronounced with a 'j' sound).

NEWSAGENTS See 'Shops'.

NEWSBOYS Paperboys, to you. These are becoming a rare breed, an endangered species, since many motorists don't see them. They are young boys between eight and fifteen who sell the daily newspapers on street corners, at intersections, and so on. They also trundle around the streets on their pushbikes delivering papers to private homes.

NICK Ah, now here's an interesting one. On the one hand it can mean condition—'It's in good nick', it's in good condition. On the other hand, it can also mean 'to steal'—'He nicked it', he stole it.

Then there's the same little word meaning a prison—'He's in the nick', he's in jail.

And if someone 'nicks into the shop' he has 'hurried in and out'.

NICKED In the same vein as jail, we suspect, since to 'be nicked' means to 'be caught'.

But if someone tells you to 'get nicked' they're being frightfully rude (use your imagination here).

51

NICK OFF Go away.

NIFTY Clever, swift, suave, nice. Nifty little word, innit?

NINCOMPOOP A nong.

NIP, NIP IN Run, run in.

NIPPERS Children.

NIPPY Cold, chilly.

NITWIT A nincompoop.

NONG A fool, an idiot.

NOODLE The head; 'Use ya noodle'.

NOSH Food. 'Nosh-up'—a meal.

NYE-NYE Goodnight. 'Nye-nyes' means sleep—'He's gone nye-nyes'.

OCKER A rough and ready, strine-speaking Australian. Earl's Court in London seems to be full of them. We've got quite a few here, too.

'OI A shout for attention.

OO'ROO Goodbye.

OPs Slang for a cigarette you get from someone else—'Other people's'.

ORRIGHT All right.

O.S. Overseas.

OUTBACK The remote parts of Australia.

OWZAT How is that? Used mostly in cricket when the team that's out ask the umpire if a batsman, who is in, is out (see 'Cricket').

OZ Short for Australia.

P

PADDY WAGON A police van; Black Maria.

PADDOCK A field.

PAIN KILLERS Now should you require a pain killer for anything (get stuck into our beer which has a much higher alcohol content than yours, and you'll definitely need one), you'll need to know the names of said medicine. The most common you can get without a doctor's prescription are: Aspro, Bex, Panadol, Codral.

PARKA A ski jacket.

PICTURES Movies. Australians, however, have the habit of pronouncing it 'pitches'. They're also called 'flicks'.

PIDDLE To urinate.

PIDDLING Small.

PIGS Like hell! Yes, the irreverent also use it as a term for police. And we are gradually dropping the term 'pigs might fly' because these days they do—most police forces have helicopters. (Sorry, officer, just joking; trying to explain a point, y'see . . .)

PINCH To steal. To 'feel the pinch' is to struggle financially.

PINCHA Short for 'pinch of manure', although a more direct description is usual. 'He's not worth a pincha'—he's not worth anything.

PINK FIT This is not pink, nor does it fit. It can mean someone will be upset by something: 'When she sees what you've done to her kitchen, she'll have a pink fit'. Or it can refer to an impossibility: 'They'll never find it in a pink fit'.

A pink fit can lead to a person going red in the face and having a blue with someone.

PLEB A common person; low-class.

PLODDER Someone who does things slowly, but surely.

PLONK Wine. It can also mean place: 'Plonk it there'—place it there.

POKIES Slot machines. New South Wales is the only state that's legally got them . . . for now.

POONCE A twit; a soppy fool.

POSH Fancy, grand, luxurious. A monied person.

PREMIER You have state governors, we have premiers. Strangely, the football team that wins the grand final (championship) is called 'the premier team'. And they say sport is non-political!

PRIMA DONNA A show-off; a glory-seeker.

PRIME MINISTER The same as your President. And like your President, he's called a lot of names, most of them impolite.

PUBLIC TOILET Should you feel the need, so to speak, when you are in the city, don't ask for the John or whatever. No, you must ask for the 'public toilet'. And, by golly, you have to pay to use some of them.

PUBLIC TRANSPORT   All major Australian cities have a suburban train network, as well as various bus services. Melbourne also has its trams (street cars), which are similar to the San Francisco cable cars, except they are electric, in different colours, and nothing like them, really.

Trains: These come in various shapes, colours, and sizes and are usually called anything except trains. They serve most suburban areas and have been known to run to the advertised timetables. They start early in the morning and run until midnight, except when they're not running due to:

- Complete electric blackout.
- Overhead wires power failure.
- Engine breakdown.
- Signal points failure.
- Strike by staff.*

Buses: These also attempt to run to a timetable and serve areas serviced by trains as well as those not serviced by trains. The hours they run are similar to that of trains, except when they're not running due to:

- Breakdowns.
- Accidents.
- Strike by staff.*

Trams: These, too, come in different shapes and sizes, and are as dependable as trains. Trams start early in the morning and run until midnight, except when they're not running due to:

- Complete electrical blackout.
- Breakdowns.
- Overhead wires power failure.
- Tram-car collision.
- Tram-tram collision.
- Strike by staff.*

* This is the most common cause of non-appearance by said vehicles.

Fares are said to be reasonable. It is usually the government that says that.

At the major stations, all trains arriving and departing are announced over a loudspeaker system. The departures, particularly, do not always coincide with those listed on the various notice-

PUBLIC TRANSPORT....!

boards and/or TV screens.

For example, you're waiting for a train to go to the suburb of, say, Balmain. The announcement comes over: 'Vsphijrk jumdoi . .nd Balmain. Xbdga r dg deparxnsd platform four.' It's that simple, but the trouble is, you're usually on platform two when that announcement is made.

Or you are about to board the train when the TV screen flashes 'Wait for announcement'. After twenty minutes, the loudspeaker crackles: 'Train to Balmain, csgjwlf moshncye msgicnf zudhdm ndus.' And you are not only waiting, you are also wondering.

The answer to all public transport problems in Australia is get a cab (see 'Taxis').

PUNCH-UP A fight.

PUNT A bet, a gamble. It is also a type of kick in Australian Rules football.

PUSH-OFF Leave.

QANTAS This is the name of Australia's international airline. It is not, as some people have believed, a marsupial, namely the koala.

QUADDY Quadrella (see 'Races').

QUEER A homosexual. We use 'queen', too.

QUID Two dollars; dates back to when we had the pound sterling in our currency.

QUIDDIT Quit it, stop it.

QUINCE See 'Poonce'. And 'It gets on my quince'—it gets on my nerves, it annoys me.

QUINELLA See 'Races'.

R

RACES When it comes to horse-racing, boy, are we big on it. The horses race clockwise or anti-clockwise, depending on which state you are in (ask a cabbie). To bet on the races, you can go to the racetrack and bet with a bookie (bookmaker), or you can go to the TAB (Totalizator Agency Board), which operates both on-course and off-course (a betting shop).

And you can take a double (pick the winners of two nominated races), a quinella (first and second in one race), a trifecta (first, second, and third in one race), or a quadrella (winners of four races).

Or you can save your money and go to the pub instead.

RACKET Noise. Yes, yes—it also means a shady deal.

RACK-OFF Leave—*now.*

RAM How can we put this delicately? Ah . . . it is used to describe a man who has many (and we mean many) conquests with women.

RAM IT Shove it; stick it.

RATBAG An idiot, a fool. Although, we suppose, one could get a bag in which to keep a rat, and call it a rat-bag. (What a ratbag idea.)

RHYMING SLANG Please be seated. This could take quite a while. You see, like the English cockney, Australians use a lot of rhyming slang. Here we list only the most common, but do remember that, in many cases, Australians shorten it from two or three words in common speech. For example, the 'rubbid y dub' (pub) becomes 'rubbidy'.

Now, are we all set? Good. Take a deep breath and away we go . . .

Frog and toad: Road.
Dad and Dave: Shave.
One another: Mother.
Cheese and kisses: Missus (wife).
Trouble and strife: Wife.
Billy lids: Kids.
China plate: Mate.

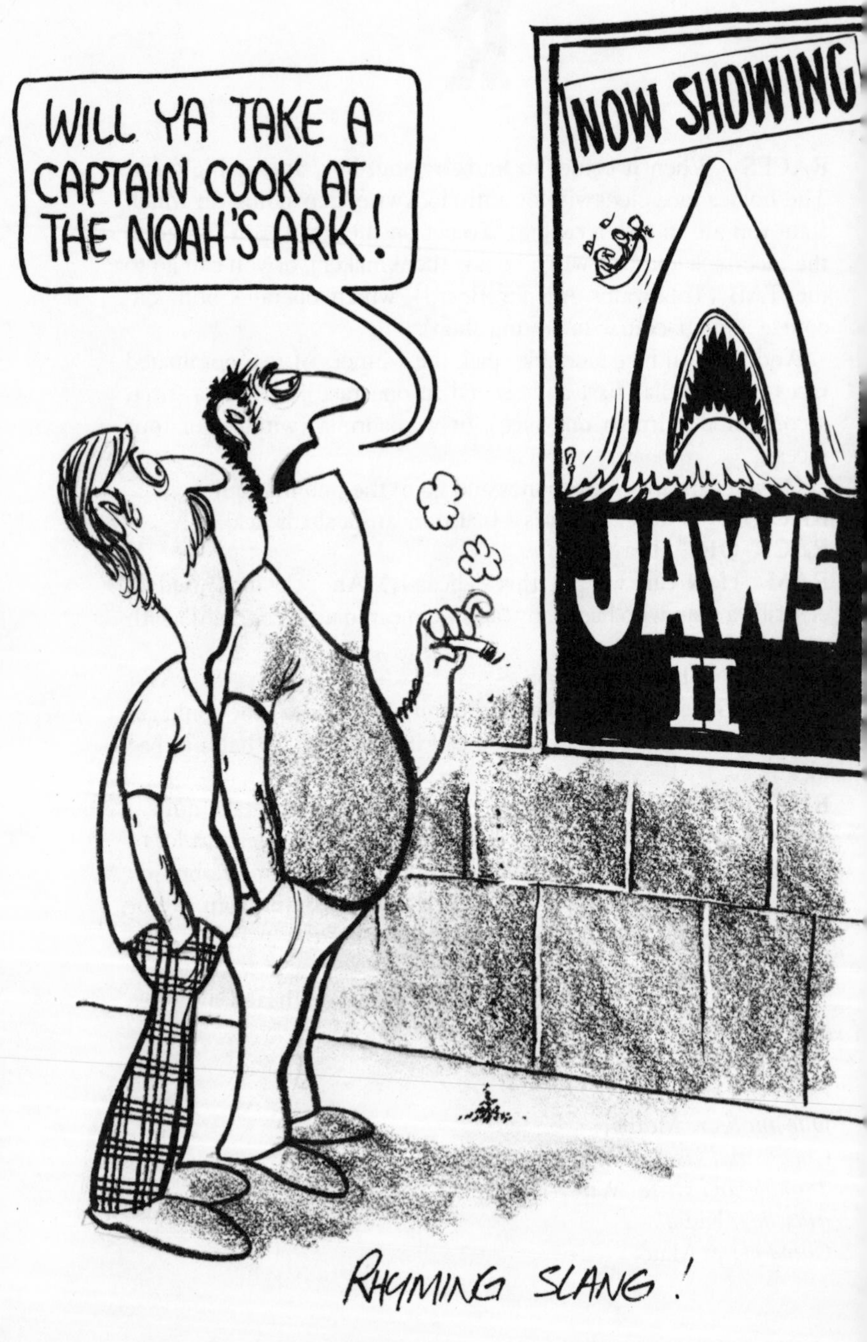
WILL YA TAKE A CAPTAIN COOK AT THE NOAH'S ARK!
NOW SHOWING
JAWS II
RHYMING SLANG!

Bib and braces: Races.

Red hots: Trots (harness racing).

Septic tank: Yank.

North and south: Mouth.

Captain Cook: Look.

Butcher's hook: Crook, ill; or crooked, as in illegal.

Dead horse: Sauce.

Dog's eye: Pie.

Eau de Cologne: Phone.

Currant bun: Sun.

John hops: Cops, police.

Armadillo: Pillow.

Aristotle: Bottle.

Tea leaf: Thief.

Tit for tat: Hat.

Elephant's trunk: Drunk.

Molly the monk: Drunk. (We drink a lot down here.)

Snake's hiss: Urinate. (Use your imagination.)

Adelaide to Gawler: Crawler—one who tries to ingratiate himself with a superior.

Soldiers bold: Cold.

Noah's Ark: Shark.

Tom-tits: Decency prevents us . . . let's just say it's for a shortened form of manure.

RICHARD   'It's had the Richard'—it's no good, it's broken.

RIGHTO   All right.

RINGER   A shearer; one who shears sheep. Also one who resembles closely another person: 'Gawd, he's a ringer for old Harry'.

RIPPER   Bewdy; great, good.

ROOT   Expletive deleted.

ROTTER   A rat (as in nasty person).

ROUTE   Pronounced 'root'.

RS   Lousy, awful. It is derived from rat . . . well, excreta. (We do hope you weren't eating.)

RUBBISH   To put someone down, usually in a light-hearted way. It is also used for garbage, or trash. And, a rubbish bin is a trash can.

RUGBY   This is the main team sport(s) played in New South Wales and most of Queensland. It is also played in other states, but on a smaller scale . . . no, this doesn't mean they use smaller players. The more astute readers will have noticed the '(s)' at the end of the word 'sport'. That's 'cos there's two of 'em — Rugby Union and Rugby League.

Rugby Union does not mean that a shop steward wanders on to the playing field every ten minutes to yell 'Everybody out'. No. In the beginning there was only Union, but late in the 1800s snobbery was apparently the cause of a breakaway movement called Rugby League.

So it became that Rugby Union was left for the gentry, and League was for the workers. League has thirteen players to a side, and Union has fifteen. We are not suggesting that there were more of the gentry than of the working class. We feel it was more than likely that the working class thought they needed fewer men to flatten the opposition.

Both codes are played on 'rectangular ovals' with two tall poles stuck in the ground at each end. Each pair of uprights has a crossbar. This is because there are several sorts of goals that can be scored.

Now, to avoid confusion, we won't try to tell you the worth of each goal or score. Suffice to say that they vary between two and three points between the codes, as well as the various types of scores in the game (clear as mud, isn't it?).

Field goals are when the ball is kicked between the poles, but above the crossbar, from the field. A conversion also has to be kicked in the same way. Well, the ball does, but when a player puts the ball on the ground behind the goal line for a 'try', it then has to be converted . . . (Dearly beloved, the football has been saved and is now earning fifteen per cent interest . . . sorry, wrong type of 'converted'.) Why it is called a 'try' may be apparent. What isn't apparent is why the conversion isn't called a 'success' or a 'tried' or . . . (Are you still there?).

Then there are penalties awarded for, among other things, a player being offside. He's still on the side (in the team), but happened to be in the wrong place at the wrong time.

To get the ball to their goals to score, a team has to move the ball forward by passing it backwards. The ball can be kicked forward, but that's when players, still on the side, can get offside.

In Rugby Union, if the ball goes out of bounds, there is a strange ritual called a 'line-out' — inside the line . . . or something. In

League, there is a scrum on such occasions.

In Union, if a player is tackled, he is supposed to let go of the ball and the game continues. In League, a tackled player hangs on to the ball for dear life until every member of the opposing side has piled on top of him.

The players are usually large, big, um . . . huge. But there are some smaller players thrown in for their speed. And if you're only average size and build and if you've got a dozen or so men, weighing over 110 kilograms each, pounding after you, you'd need to be fast.

It should be noted that much rougher tackling (which has nothing to do with fishing) is allowed than in Aussie Rules. Among the few things banned are forearm jolts, punching (which everyone does, anyway), stiff-arm tackles, and dangerous play which includes piledrivers.

A piledriver is not a large machine which is trundled on to the ground from time to time. Rather, it's when a player picks up an opponent, turns him upside down, and rams him head first into the ground.

But the referee has the power to send players off the ground if he thinks they have been naughty boys. (Wait, don't go away—it gets better).

That's the game, roughly. And the players, roughly. Now, roughly, the spectators, or supporters, who are much the same as supporters of various sporting teams Australia-over.

They call the referee endearing names like 'mongrel' and 'swine' and 'bluddy mugs' and 'expletive deleteds'. They call players from the opposing sides much the same things.

And in support of their team, in an effort to encourage the players, they chant things like 'avago yabluddy mug, but' and 'geddin there an' kill the so-and-so, but'.

There, that wasn't so hard to follow, was it? However, if you are in some doubt, may we suggest the usual . . . buy a proper rule book, or go to the pub.

RUMBLE A fight.

RUMPUS A noise, a disturbance.

RUNNERS Sneakers. Also serious, two-legged creatures who claim they are getting fit.

S

SAMMIDGE, SAMMICH, SANGER A sandwich.

SAP A sucker; one easily led.

SAUCE Our tomato sauce is your ketchup, except that tomato ketchup is now available here.

SCONE The human head; also what you call a biscuit; pronounced 'Scon'.

SCREAMER Now you may find this hard to believe, but this does not refer to someone who races around screaming. It is used in reference to an outstanding event, such as a mark in football (a mark is the art of catching the football in the air). If a player jumps high into the air and marks the ball over his head, he is said to have 'taken a screamer'.

SHAT OFF Browned off, fed up.

SHEILAH Another word for girl or woman.

SHIDDAY Oh gosh, or big deal!

SHIDDY Lousy.

SHIN To climb. 'Shin up that tree'—climb up that tree.

SHONKY Poorly made.

SHOPS, SHOPPING Ah, shopping, one of the most uncivilised aspects of Australian life. Here, most shops open between 8 a.m. and 9 a.m., and close between 5.30 p.m. and 6 p.m., on weekdays. Some stores, such as Safeway, department stores, and various smaller stores, stay open until 9 p.m. Thursdays and Fridays. This is known as 'late-night shopping'. Perhaps, if 10 p.m. closing is ever introduced, it will be known as 'early morning shopping'!

Some larger food chain stores also stay open a little later—7 p.m. or 8 p.m.—on Wednesday nights in some states . . . the adventurous little devils.

Saturday mornings, most stores open at their normal times and close at (wait for it) . . . midday! But again, some stores in some states, such as K Mart, keep their variety stores open until 1 p.m. and their food stores open until 5 p.m.—(Ah, such bliss).

Sundays; well, Sundays are a bit of a bother. It's considered very naughty in some states to open on Sundays. Milk bars are a

SHOPS AND SHOPPING HOURS...

different kettle of fish, you must understand (see 'Milk Bars'). In Victoria, for example, many areas allow you to open your store if you sell books, but will rap you over the knuckles and drag you off to court on the ever-so-serious charge of illegal trading if you have a hardware store daring to open on the Sabbath.

To confuse the issue even further, there are areas where it doesn't matter a tinker's cuss (look it up, look it up) what sort of store you have, you can open all day Sunday.

There are very few twenty-four hour stores. The occasional Seven-Eleven store is open all the time, but many are just as the name implies . . . open from 7 a.m. to 11 p.m. Food-Plus is another store operating on the same lines.

Banks are open for business at 10 a.m. and close at 3 p.m. on weekdays, except Fridays when they close at 5 p.m. They don't open at all on weekends.

Service stations, as in garages or gas stations, will have the odd twenty-four hour outlet, but generally they close any time between 6 p.m. and 10 p.m. Some stay open until midnight, then hung up their pumps for another day.

We also have various 'personalised shops'. Marvellous places, really, specialising in just one product. For example, we still have butcher shops where you can buy only meat (lovely, fresh stuff it is, too); and greengrocers (usually called fruit shops) where one buys all their fruit and vegetables. Some shops specialise in cheese; others in continental foods, and so on.

Then there are newsagents. This is where you buy your newspapers, magazines, all stationery, lottery tickets, books, greeting cards, gift-wrapping, and what-have-you.

Take-away food stores (food-to-go) differ somewhat. There are the McDonalds and Kentucky Fried and so on, but we also have our English style fish-and-chip shops. Here one pays a reasonable price for fried or grilled fish and potato chips (fries) wrapped in paper. Some shops still use newspaper and this always gives the meal that extra something. One can also give the old taste buds an extra treat by including a potato cake or scallop—a large, flat slice of potato fried in batter.

Of course there are pizza shops with take-away, but here one has to order a whole pizza. The ordering of just one slice or two is unheard of. Chinese restaurants also have a take-away food service and this is always referred to as 'chow food'.

Delicatessens and milk bars provide hot meat pies (with, of course, sauce), sandwiches, hot dogs (again with sauce), and the like, when you have to eat on the run.

SHOUSE Lavatory (see under 'L'). Also, something can be described as 'shouse' (awful).

SHOVE OFF Leave.

SHOW PONY A show-off.

SIC As in 'sic him'—go get him.

SITTER A certainty; something that is easy.

SLAMMER Jail.

SKITE A bragger; to brag, to boast.

SLOPS Beer. 'He got stuck into the slops'—he had a lot to drink.

SLOSHED Drunk.

SLOUCH Slow. Usually used in the opposite sense: 'he's no slouch'—he's not slow, or not silly.

SLY GROG With Australians being great drinkers and Australia's crazy liquor laws, if you run out of grog on a Sunday there is always a sly grog 'shop' somewhere. This is where you can get beer (illegally) and for a higher price than normal. Information on the whereabouts of sly grog can be obtained (sometimes) from the drinkers at the local pub; better still, ask a cabbie.

SMASHED Drunk.

SMOKO (or smokho) Coffee break.

SMOUSH, SMOUCH To kiss. Derived from 'smooch'.

SNAGS Sausages.

SNAKES Abbreviated form of rhyming slang for urinating: 'Snakes hiss'.

SNARKY Short-tempered, snappy.

SNIFTER Usually refers to cold weather—'snifter weather'.

SNORT A drink. 'Ya cummin down tootha pub t'avva snort?'

SNOT Apart from the awfully obvious, it also means to punch someone on the nose—'I'll snot him.'

SO-AND-SO Usually inserted instead of an expletive deleted: 'You rotten so-and-so'. Can also refer to an indefinite item.

SOFT DRINK Soda pop.

SOOK A cry-baby.

SORDA Sort of.

'SORF Leave—immediately, if not sooner.

SORT Good looking woman: 'She's a good sort'.

SOUP Trouble: 'He's in the soup'—he's in trouble.

SPELLING You will probably have noticed by now, astute little devils that you are, that although we talk differently to you—or you to us—we all speak English. And write it. And most words are spelt the same. But there are a few where we differ.

For example, the word 'tire' (your spelling) as in those round rubber things on car wheels, is spelt 'tyre' here. We spell tire, as in weary, the same as you do.

Then there are words like 'center' and 'fiber', which we spell 'centre' and 'fibre'.

And, of course, a tennis racket here means some shady dealings in the sport. We spell it 'racquet'.

Now let's talk about money. You may very well write a check for $200 or so—we write a cheque.

We can hear you asking why there is such a difference . . . Can you hear us saying we don't know?

SPIDER Apart from those creepy-crawlies (see 'Wildlife'), this is also a drink consisting of lemonade poured over icecream and then stirred. Other flavour drinks can be used. (No, the place hasn't really gone stark raving mad.)

SPOGGY A sparrow (bird).

SPORTS Name a sport and, short of something like homing Mongolian butterfly racing, it's a fair bet that you'll find it in Australia. (You'll also find someone running a book on it, too!)

The major sports are thoroughbred horse racing, trotting (harness racing), greyhound racing (the animals always win, by the way), tennis, golf, cricket, rugby, basketball, lawn bowls, and Australian Rules football.

In the case of the latter, it's almost a religion in South Australia, Western Australia, and Tasmania. In Victoria it *is* a religion. It's also pretty big in Queensland, the Northern Territory, the Australian Capital Territory, and attracts a reasonable interest in New South Wales where many people seem to prefer the strange sports of Rugby League and Rugby Union (which see).

The most famous Australian Rules football club is Collingwood, also known as the Magpies. It has the most supporters—who also happen to be the most fanatical.

You may not believe it (we find it hard ourselves) but when Collingwood wins, daily newspaper sales go up. When they lose . . . oh, and . . . er . . . Collingwood last won the premiership (or

66

championship) in 1958, so please be careful—particularly in Melbourne—what you say about the Mighty Magpies.

But, getting back to other sports, you'll also find baseball, archery, darts, pool, swimming, track and field athletics, yachting, boxing, wrestling (Actors' Equity have been known to take an interest in this), shooting, table tennis, weightlifting, rowing, motor racing (what oil shortage?), squash, racquet (sorry, racket) ball and . . . oh, a whole host of you-name-it-we've-got-it sports.

Well, we do have one other, but most true Australians don't usually sing its praises. It's soccer, which has a huge following, and which is generally referred to as 'that round-ball game' or 'wog-ball'.

Yes . . . we may be multi-cultural, but we're also multi-intolerant!

STARKERS   Naked, nude.

STATES   Australia has six states, and two territories. The states are: Victoria (which it is in its attitude to many things), New South Wales (even though it isn't new and it has nothing to do with Wales), Queensland, Western Australia (which it is), and South Australia (although two other states are further south than it), and Tasmania (one of the states further south), which is known as the Apple Isle—because it is an island, and they grow apples down there; they also grow good football players.

Most states, or their inhabitants, have a nickname: Victoria—Yarra Yabbies; South Australia—Crow-eaters; Western Australia—Sand Gropers; Queensland—Banana Benders; New South Wales—well, they don't really have one—Melbourne people hope that if they ignore Sydney, it will go away; Tasmania—Tasmaniacs, although this is not used very much because people from Tasmania get very upset very easily.

The territories are: The Northern Territory, which has now gained state rights and may one day be in a right state (if you get the drift); and the Australian Capital Territory, centred around the Australian capital city named Canberra where Federal Parliament is (it is a bit like Washington D.C. and Congress and the Senate). The Prime Minister's residence, The Lodge (that's your White House) is there, too. Its greatest exports are hot air, unpopular decisions, and retired politicians.

All eastern states—Queensland, New South Wales, Victoria, and Tasmania—are in the same time zone, except in summer when all except Queensland switch to summer time, or daylight saving.

67

There is a saying that the reason Queensland does not switch is because the Premier, Mr Joh Bjelke-Petersen, believes the sun shines out of him, and he's not getting out of bed an hour earlier for anyone. We know it is really because Queensland has a sunny climate anyway.

South Australia and the Northern Territory are half an hour behind the eastern states (time-wise), and Western Australia is two hours behind.

If we were asked to very briefly summarise the states, we would probably do it thus:

Western Australia: Big, hot, mines, small towns, and cyclones. (Actually, an American comedian visiting the state capital of Perth was once asked what he thought of Perth. He replied: 'It's nice—but isn't it a long way from the city?')

South Australia: Churches, industry, primary produce, nice weather, and lack of nightlife.

New South Wales: King's Cross, Rugby, League's clubs, primary produce, industry, nice weather, pokies, and busy.

Northern Territory: Big, hot, mines, desert, cattle stations, cyclones, and Alice Springs and Ayers Rock.

Queensland: Hot, rich people on holidays or in retirement, pineapples, and peanuts. (There have been cases of people not knowing the difference between the peanuts and politicians.)

Victoria: Dreadful weather (particularly in Melbourne, not so in Mildura), primary produce, Aussie Rules, trams, industry, and busy.

Tasmania: Apples, football players, cold, and unbusy.

Australian Capital Territory: Politicians, public servants, cold but with a lot of hot air.

That's what we would say if we were going to give a very brief summary of each state or territory. But it might start arguments, so we won't.

STINK Trouble, a fight.

STINKER Yes, well, a stinker is a person who is a real rotter, a louse, a rat. But a day can be a stinker, too. If things have gone wrong at work, your day has been a stinker. If it is very hot, it is a stinker—'it's a stinker of a day', 'it's stinkin' hot'.

STONE Among other things, this is how we once measured people's weight (before metrication). For example, a person you would describe as weighing 256 pounds, we described as being

18 stone 4 pounds. More often than not, however, we describe them as 'bluddy fat'. (For mathematicians: a stone equals 14 pounds.)

STOUSH A fight.

STRIKE ME Dear reader, do be careful with this. If someone says to you 'strike me', unless you have a death wish or want to spend part of your vacation in hospital—don't (strike him, that is). He simply means, 'Well, I'll be . . .'.

STRINE This is sometimes spoken *of* in hushed, reverent tones. It is usually spoken *in* a raucous, irreverent manner. Because 'this' is strine, the 'official' language spoken by many Australians. The greatest exponents of strine are known affectionately (and otherwise) as Ockers.

Ockers run words together, clip some words short, mispronounce some, speak at a rapid rate, and generally are impossible to understand unless you are another Australian.

Observe the following: 'Owyagoing, orright? Cummindown tootha pubtava beearorwot? Beena bonzadye, annit. Me missa sad egg nishnin puddin thouse yesty. Dunnarf maika diffrence. Jasee the foodyon teev lar snight? . . .' Well, you get the idea.

Except you have no idea what that was all about, do you? Translated it was: 'How are you going, all right? Coming down to the pub to have a beer, or what? Been a bonzer day, hasn't it? My missus [wife] had air conditioning put in the house yesterday. Doesn't half make a difference. Did you see the footy on TV last night?'

The art for much of strine, which is natural for Australians and impossible for anyone else, is to leave off the end of one word and use it to start the next word. Hence 'last night' becomes 'lar snight'. Or to run the words together as in 'thouse' is 'the house' joined, so to speak.

Isn't this fun? Wouldn't you all like to be able to speak strine? Wouldn't that be great? It would be the end of civilisation, that's what it would be.

STROPPY Short-tempered.

STRUTH, STREWTH Gosh.

STUBBY We really do hate to be confusing, but these are a pair of shorts, and also a small bottle of beer. The usual size of a bottle of beer is 750 millilitres; a stubby is about half that—for small people who aren't very thirsty!

70

STUFF IT   The hell with it.
SWAGGIE, SWAGGY   A hobo.
SWEETS   Lollies, candy. Can also be dessert (see 'Eating out').

T

TA   Thanks.

TAP   Faucet. (Did you hear about the tap dancer? He fell into the sink and broke his legs.)

TART   Apart from being a sweet pastry, this also refers to a wanton woman (usually wanton, but not gettin').

TATTS   One of the several lotteries that operate in Victoria. Yes folks, for just $1 you could win $25 000! And that's just the first prize.

TAXIS   These are cabs. In Australia, it is customary for a man travelling alone to sit in the front seat with the driver. Most women prefer to sit in the back seat.

The reason for the lone man to sit in the front is that the driver is less likely to think there will be trouble—that he is going to be robbed—than if a man sits in the back seat. Or he may think you're a snotty-nosed poonce (see under 'P') if you sit in the back.

Incidentally, he's not being rude if he tells you to belt up. He's likely to say it even if you haven't opened your mouth. He's just telling you to fasten the seat belt, since it is now compulsory to wear seat belts in the front and the back seats of a car.

Like cab drivers the world over, they are likely to leave you pale and shaking at your destination after a demonstration of their driving skills.

But if there is *anything* you want to know about *anything*, just ask the cabbie. They know everything. Ask 'em—they'll tell you.

TEA   The evening meal. Dinner, to you.

TEA-LEAF   Thief (see 'Rhyming slang').

TEEV   Television. Also 'telly'.

TELEGRAM   A cable or wire (Western Union and all that!)

TAXIS / DRIVING

TINKER'S CUSS 'He's not worth a tinker's cuss'—he's not worth anything.

TINNY A can of beer.

TIP A dump; a rubbish tip, where all trash is dumped.

TIPPING Are you sitting down for this? You don't have to tip in Australia! You can, but only if you think the person deserves it, and only what you think it is worth. One thing—don't leave a tip on the table for a waiter or waitress—hand it to them. Leave it on the table and someone will knock it off—that is to say, steal it.

TIPPLE A quiet drink.

TITFA Tit-for-tat—an eye for an eye. Also rhyming slang for 'hat'.

TOGS Clothing for sporting activities, such as a swimming costume (bathers).

TOMMYROT 'He's talking tommyrot'—he's talking rubbish.

TOURS Oh, there are dozens of these, taking in pioneer villages, the mountains, museums, country towns, rivers, snow resorts, and so on. Ask your travel agent—or a cabbie.

TRAM CONDUCTOR Although one or two have been known to stand in the middle of the road, tap their batons, then lead the trams through a moving rendition of 'Charge of the Light Brigade', that is not their function. They are on the trams to collect the fares.

TRAMS See 'Public transport'.

TRANNY A portable radio; short for 'transistor'.

TRAPS Police.

TREDDLY Bicycle; also 'Deadly Treddly'.

TRUCKIE Trucker.

TRUNDLE To trundle something, to wheel something.

TUCKER Food.

TWO-UP You will speak in hushed and revered tones when you mention two-up. This is Australia's traditional and national gambling game. It's also illegal in most places. Basically it is betting on whether two coins will come up heads or tails after being thrown into the air by the spinner. For full details ask a cabbie. But be polite.

TYRE Tire.

'ULLO Hello.
UMP, UMPY An umpire.
UNDIES Underwear; also called 'underdaks'.
UPPIT, UPPYA The hell with it (or you).
UPPITY Snobbish.
USETA Used to.

VEGEMITE This is a thick, black yeast extract—and it is lovely, particularly on buttered toast. Some Australians can't live without it—to the point of taking some with them while on vacation. Most Americans we know don't like it. Some do. So try it . . . please!

WAG A comedian, a practical joker.
WAKKA A fool, someone who makes a silly mistake.
WALKABOUT This originally referred to the Aborigines' habit of packing up every so often and moving camp. Now it applies to anyone who wanders off somewhere, usually without telling where they are going.

WALLOP   To hit.
WALLOPERS   Police.
WARDA   Water.
WATERING HOLE   A hotel or pub: 'The local watering hole'.
WEETIES   Good little bit of brekky (breakfast) nosh this. Lovely, wholesome wheat flakes! Quite right, it's a breakfast cereal, but it is also used as a term for strength.

If someone's strength is flagging, a friend might say: 'Didn't have our Weeties this morning then?' Or the person themselves will say: 'Not enough Weeties!' This little snippet has already livened up your day, hasn't it?

WHACKED   Drunk; hit; tired.
WHOPPA   (Whopper) Big: 'Boy, whatta whoppa'. And a lie is sometimes called 'a whoppa'.
WILDLIFE   Australia has a lot of unique wildlife, the majority of which you'll have a better chance of seeing by going to the zoo than by going bush.

Kangaroo: Contrary to popular belief, they are *not* found in main streets.

Dingo: And they don't eat babies.

Wallaby: Like a kangaroo.

Wombat: Eats roots and leaves (now, be nice).

Koala: Not a bear. Please note that. Everyone calls them 'koala bears'—they're not, they're marsupials, bad-tempered marsupials.

Platypus: There is no flatterpus than a platypus—but it doesn't mattermus.

Possum: Yes, they play dead.

Emu: A rather large bird that can't fly. But, boy, can they run.

Then there are the more mundane ones like foxes, water buffalo, flying possums, alligators, crocodiles, cockatoos, galahs, rabbits, hares, top-knot pigeons, wedge-tailed eagles, hawks, carpet snakes, goannas, lizards—nothing to worry about.

But speaking of snakes, the ones to avoid are taipans, brown, black, and tiger snakes and copperheads. (Ladies should also avoid the 'trouser snake'.)

And steer clear of these spiders—red-back, black widow, and funnel webs. Nasty little (?) creatures, they are.

WOOP-WOOP   Non-existent place used to describe a shanty town a million miles from nowhere.

X

Nothing for this letter. It never was very exciting, anyway.

Y

YABBIES Crawfish, to you.

YAHOO No, nobody is cheering. A yahoo is a slob, a loud-mouthed fool.

YAKKA Work; 'hard yakka'. This is something a bludger will never be guilty of.

YAK-YAK Talk incessantly.

YARECK'N Do you reckon? Do you think so?

YOBBO A yahoo.

Z

ZACK A five cent piece (from the days of the sixpenny piece).

ZONK A dud.

ZONKED Tired; fell asleep.

Z We know that you know that this is simply a letter of the alphabet. But Australians pronounce it 'zed', not 'zee' as you do. So now you know . . . Zed—the last word in alphabets!

EPILOGUE

You've got this far, have you? It was painless after all, wasn't it? And isn't it all we said it would be? Don't you now know everything you wanted to know about Australia? As if we would lie to you!

And it has really made you want to visit us here Down Under, hasn't it?

So if you still haven't paid the cashier, please do so now.*

The authors need the money . . . to pay for a trip to America.

* It's either that or we write a second book about . . . 'Great Tea-Leaves We Have Known' . . .